AF001

MASSIMILIANO AFIERO

AXIS FORCES 1

WW2 AXIS FORCES

The Axis Forces 001 - First edition February 2017 by Soldiershop.com.
Cover & Art Design by soldiershop factory. ISBN code: 978-88-93272063
First published by Soldiershop, copyright © 2017 Soldiershop (BG) ITALY. No part of this publication may be reproduced, stored in a retrieval system or transmitted by any form or by any means, electronic, recording or otherwise without the prior permission in writing from the publishers. The publisher remains to disposition of the possible having right for all the doubtful sources images or not identifies. Visit www.soldiershop.com to read more about all our books and to buy them.

In merito alla specifica serie Italia storia ebook serie Ritterkreuz l'editore Soldiershop informa che non essendone l'autore ne il primo editore del materiale pervenuto dall'associazione Ritterkreuz, declina ogni responsabilità in merito al suo contenuto di testi e/o immagini e la sua correttezza. A tal proposito segnaliamo che la pubblicazione Ritterkreuz tratta esclusivamente argomenti a carattere storico-militare e non intende esaltare alcun tipo di ideologia politica presente o del passato cosi come non intende esaltare alcun tipo di regime politico del secolo precedente ed alcuna forma di razzismo.

Note editoriali dell'edizione cartacea

The Axis Forces number 1 – January 2017

Direction and editing
Via San Giorgio, 11 – 80021 AFRAGOLA (NA) -ITALY
Managing and Chief Editor: Massimiliano Afiero
Email: maxafiero@libero.it
Website: www.maxafiero.it

Contributors
Stefano Canavassi, Carlos Caballero Jurado, Rene Chavez, Antonio Guerra, John B. Köser, Lars Larsen, Christophe Leguérandais, Erik Norling, Scott Revell, Raphael Riccio, Charles Trang, Cesare Veronesi, Sergio Volpe

Editorial

Here we are again to present a new magazine dedicated to the history of the Axis formations during the Second World War, with most of the same group of employees who previously were involved in producing the magazine 'The European Volunteer'. We hope that this new project will be positively received by our readers, who already subscribed to the previous magazine so that we can continue our research and our studies on this particular subject of the Second World War, focusing our attention primarily on foreign voluntary formations of the Axis, but also expanding our discussion to the national military units of Germany, Italy and other European satellite states. Send us your comments and your impressions, so you can meet your needs and improve the content of our magazine. Wishing everyone a pleasant reading experience, see you all in the next issue.

Massimiliano Afiero

The publication of The Axis Forces deals exclusively with subjects of a historical military nature and is not intended to promote any type of political ideology either present or past, as it also does not seek to exalt any type of political regime of the past century or any form of racism.

Contents

April 1941: SS motorcyclists in Belgrade
by Charles Trang

SS-Hstuf. **Fritz Klingenberg.**

August Zehender with the *Ritterkreuz.*

Amongst the feats of arms of the *Waffen SS* one of the most known is clearly the conquest of Belgrade by a fistful of motorcyclists headed by *SS-Hstuf.* Fritz Klingenberg. The majority of historians focused on the audacious coup but this wouldn't have been possible without the preliminary bombing by the *Luftwaffe* nor without the threat of the imminent arrival in the Jugoslav capital of the units from the SS *"Reich"* and *11th Panzer Divisions*. The photo reportage we are proposing shows how the motorcyclist battalion of the *Reich* reached the city by… waterway.

The SS Kradschützen-Bataillon "Reich"

On the 22nd of February 1941, the *SS-FHA* ordered the formation of a motorcyclist battalion for the SS division "*Reich*", from which the 2nd SS "*Das Reich*" later originated. It's interesting to find that this new battalion was formed from the *SS-Totenkopf-Standarte 11*, a unit consisting of personnel previously in charge of prison camps but re-designated as *SS-Infanterie-Regiment 11* at the moment of being integrated in the *Reich* Division, this to compensate the loss of the "*Germania*" Regiment, transferred on December 1940 to the newly formed "*Wiking*" Division. In this month of February 1941, the *Reich* Division was quartered in the region of Vesoul, France. The headquarters staff off the new battalion was formed in Vitrey from Stab I./SS-IR 11; the 1st Kompanie was constituted at Vernois from the transformation of the 15.Kp./SS-IR "Deutschland"; the 2nd Kompanie was formed the same way at Rosières but from the 15.Kp/SS-IR "Der Führer"; the 3rd Kompanie, based at Betoncourt, was the former 3.Kp/SS-Aufkl.-Abt. "Reich"; the 4th Kompanie, which was in Pisseloup, was formed from the previously named 4.Kp./SS-IR 11 just like the 5th Kompanie, based at Ouge, that was originally the 1.Kp./SS-IR 11. The Battalion command was assigned to an officer that had served almost all his military career before the war in the "Deutschland" Regiment. He was the SS-Sturmbannführer August Zehender, who officially took office on the 10th of March 1941. Seen as an irreproachable officer by his superiors, he didn't have the look of the archetype of the Aryan proposed by the National-Socialist propaganda. With Brown hair, dark skin, bushy eyebrows and the eyes with a slight almond shape, he didn't look much like the majority of the members of the Division. Nevertheless, he imposed himself by the strength of his character and his conduct on the battlefield during the French campaign, when he was the commander of the *SS-Fla-MG-Abteilung*. On December 1940, he was assigned to the command post of *I./SS-IR 11*, replacing *SS-Sturmbannführer* Kurt Eimann, judged unfit to lead an Infantry Battalion. A distinguished horseman, having won many equestrian competitions, in March 1942, he was logically transferred to the *SS-Kavallerie Brigade*. Decorated with the Knight Cross with Oak Leaves, he fell during combat in February 1945 in Budapest as commander of the *22.SS-Freiwillingen-Kavalerie-Division "Maria Theresia"*.

SS-Stubaf. **Wilhelm Kment.**

SS-Ustuf. **Fritz Klingenberg.**

The first company of the Battalion was entrusted to the *SS-Hstuf.* Wilhelm Kment. Opposite to Zehender, Kment was the archetype of the Prussian Officer: his hair was so blond that it looked almost white, clear eyes, an imposing figure and a blade shaped mouth. For a soldier with such a great initiative spirit it was almost natural to be commissioned with the headquarters of the motorcyclist's *15.Kompanie* of the *"Deutschland"* Regiment. Enrolled as a volunteer, he joined the SS in 1934 as a soldier and seven year later was *Hauptsturmführer*. On the 14th of October 1941, he took command of the division's reconnaissance section replacing Johannes Mühlenkamp, wounded in combat. He himself was later wounded in action and assigned to the *SS-Junkerschule* of Bad Tölz as an instructor before serving in Himmler's General Staff as officer in charge of decorations and awards.

SS-Stubaf. **Christian Tychsen.**

The *2.Kompanie* of the motorcyclist battalion was under command of *SS-Hauptsturmführer* Fritz Klingenberg. Contrary to the previous two officers, Klingenberg belonged to a number of different units before the war, from *Leibstandarte*, Regiment *Deutschland* and *Germania*, to the inspectorate of *SS-Verfügunstruppe*. In September 1939, he was assigned as adjutant (IIa) to the *Panzerdivision "Kempf"* before taking command of the *15.(Kradsch.)Kp/SS-IR "Der Führer"* from the 1st of August 1940. One year later exactly he replaced Zehender as the Battalion commander. In April 1942, after a serious illness, he was transferred to Bad Tölz as an instructor, to return then briefly to the Division in July 1943 and subsequently assuming command of the famous *SS-Junkerschule* in March 1944. He was killed in action in January 1945, while in command of the *17.SS-Pz.Gren.Div. Götz "von Berlichingen"*.

SS motorcyclists 'Reich', April 1941.

The race for Belgrade, April 1941.

The *3.Kompanie* of the Battalion was assigned to the *SS-Hauptsturmführer* Christian Tychsen, a "clone" in physical appearance of Wilhelm Kment. He was without doubt a fine soldier with excellent qualities: energetic, conscientious but daring as well. Before the war he served in the *"Germania"* Regiment, as an anti-tank and reconnaissance officer. He took command of the Battalion in April 1942, replacing Klingenberg, then from autumn '42 was assigned to the *II./SS-Pz.rgt.2*. He was killed in action on the 28th of July 1944 at Gavray, while in command of the *SS-Panzer-Regiment 2* and of the entire *"Das Reich"* Division on a temporary basis.

The *4.Kompanie* of the Battalion was assigned to a recently promoted officer, *SS-Untersturmführer* Gerhard Hinze. Although he didn't have as brilliant a military career when compared to the other company commanders, he died during combat action on the 20th of August 1944 in Normandy as commander of the *3.Kp./SS-Pz.Aufkl.-Abt.10.*

The *5.Kompanie* was commanded by *SS-Ostuf.* Joachim Wüstenberg. This officer was born in Guatemala and, contrary to the others, was not coming from the *SS-Verfügungs-Division* but from the *Totenkopf* where he has been serving as platoon commander in the *9.Kp./SS-T.IR 2*. He too was killed in action in August 1941 in the Jelnja sector. As per the general organization of the Battalion, the first three companies were motorcyclists ones, the fourth a machine gun company and the fifth was designated "heavy" because it included one infantry gun (*I.G.*), an anti-tank (*Pak*) and a pioneer platoon.

in World War Two 1939-1945

The Balkan war

On the 31st of March 1941, the Battalion left Haute Savoie heading to the Donaueschingen Region via Belfort. Despite some difficulties with fuel supply, the unit reached Munich on the 2nd of April and on the 4th crossed the Hungarian border. Two days later it was in Arad, Romania. The following day all the units regrouped in the sector north of Temesvar. It has been planned for the Division to attack with the bulk of the forces the position of Satul Mic, from both sides, eight kilometres south-west of Denta, towards Alibunar, Pancevo and the bridge on the Danube that led to Belgrade. Some elements were to be left as a rear guard around Vrsac. On the 9th of April, at about 11am, some patrols from the Motorcyclist Battalion and the Reconnaissance Group crossed the Romanian-Hungarian border without encountering much of a resistance. Soon they contacted the other units to warn that the roads were not suitable for passage by the other vehicles. The Division then sent an engineer unit to solve the problem but

The divisional commander Paul Hausser with *Adjutant SS-Hstuf*. Weidinger and *SS-Ustuf*. Hinze, commander of 4th Company, Motorcycle Battalion, cross the Danube.

this would have needed some time. The *XXXXI.Armee-Korps*, to which the *"Reich"* Division was subordinated, issued orders for the following day to be transmitted to the various units: the Motorcyclist Battalion had the task to reach Alibunar and follow up at the head of the Division to conquer the bridge on the Danube with a quick coup. On the 11th of April, Good Friday, at 09:05hrs the Division attacked.

Despite the marshy ground, the units advanced quickly. The vehicles dove into the mud, the men proceeded on foot. Around 15:15hrs the canal south of Sv. Jovan was crossed: the road to Alibunar was finally opened. By 17:30hrs the town was within reach of the *"Deutschland"* Regiment. Until then the enemy resistance had been practically non-existent. But to conquer Alibunar the SS had to fight hard. *SS-Hstuf*. Paul Rode was among the firsts to fall under enemy fire that day.

Around 20:00hrs all the sector was secured and the Motorcyclist Battalion received the order to exploit this occasion. The following day, just after 09:00hrs, Pancevo was conquered by

Kampfgruppe "Keller" (composed of cyclists from the "*Deutschland*" Regiment) and by August Zehender's Battalion. The north shore of the Danube was soon after reached. The two units asked then the authorisation to cross the river, where it looked like there were no defending enemies deployed.

The *SS-Kradschützen-Bataillon 'Reich'* arriving in Pancevo, 12 April, at about 9:10, with the *Kampfgruppe* of *SS-Hstuf*. **Baldur Keller.**

On board vessels of various types, the Battalion motorcyclists reached Belgrade on April 16, four days after the action by Klingenberg.

SS Motorcyclists aboard a commandeered boat. Note that the battalion was at that time not attached to Division *'Reich'* but the Regiment *'Grossdeutschland'*, the famous German army's elite units.

The *SS-Hstuf.* Wilhelm Kment, at left, supervises the embarkation of his Company.

Four men are needed to take on the side-car: it was true that a *BMW R75* or *Zündapp KS750* weighed at least 670 kg!

Yugoslavia capitulated on April 18. This photo was taken two days later, when the fighting had already ended in the Belgrade area.

The *1.Kompanie* of *SS-Hstuf*. Wilhelm Kment sails on the Danube in the direction of Belgrade.

But the headquarters of the *XXXXI.Armee-Korps* had decided to give some rest to the troops before launching the final assault against the Yugoslav Capital. As a matter of fact, after the march through the marshes of Margita-Seleus-Alibunar sector the men were exhausted. Anyway, even before the negative answer from the headquarters reached the motorcyclist battalion, Fritz Klingenberg took the personal decision to go and have a look on the opposite shore. He seized a small motorboat and headed to Belgrade, accompanied by just 10 men. The following is known. Once in the city, Klingenberg went to the German Embassy to meet the *Wehrmacht* military attaché, *Oberst* Toussaint. Thanks to him, Klingenberg managed to meet the *Major* of Belgrade.

MG 34 machine guns in the air-raid. Contrary to what you may think, the Yugoslav air force was not totally absent from the skies: when the *Reich* came to Temesvar April 7, it suffered heavy bombing.

Photography often incorrectly described: as you can see these are not Kurt Meyer's scouts crossing the Gulf of Patras!

The *1.Kompanie*, piled on board a single vessel. It would seem unlikely that it could take on all of its vehicles.

The local civilian population looks at the curious spectacle of troops being ferried on requisitioned boats.

To be able to take on much material as possible, two boats were united with the wooden plates on which the motorbikes were arranged.

It 's time to land on the southern bank of the Danube, a task more difficult than boarding.

During this encounter, Fritz Klingenberg succeeded in obtaining the surrender of the capital, threatening more and heavier bombing from the *Luftwaffe*.. It was 18:45hrs. One thousand soldiers from the Yugoslav Royal Army were to be made prisoners by a handful of SS. During the night, the forward elements of the *11.Panzerdivision* entered in the city, finalising the conquest of Belgrade.

Civilians are forced to lend a hand. Some soldiers, including a nurse, have already set foot on the ground.

Motorcyclists go through a district of the city devastated by the bombs of the *Luftwaffe*.

The German bombings caused numerous victims among the civilian population.

in World War Two 1939-1945

The *1.Kompanie* quickly reach the city center to join Fritz Klingenberg.

SS-Hstuf. Klingenberg talking with *Waffen SS Kriegsberichter* about his audacious thrust on Belgrade, April 17, 1941.

A great media operation

The successful coup by Fritz Klingenberg, a daring operation indeed, was full of risks. But it was quite clear that the city garrison didn't have much intention to oppose a fierce resistance in a battle that all considered already lost. It would have been overwhelmed by the armoured and motorised units that invested the capital just after the formal surrender from the north and the south. Furthermore, they had to think about the civil population and try to spare them more suffering: the inhabitants of Belgrade having already paid a high tribute under the *Luftwaffe* massive bombings. Klingenberg succeeded in obtaining a surrender that the city's mayor had already prepared.

This coup had the undoubted merit of saving many human lives but certainly it was not the decisive action, as it was later described by the Third Reich's propaganda. For Himmler was an unexpected opportunity: making of Klingenberg a National Hero, recruitment in the SS reached one of its peaks, with them acquiring the image of elite units full of courage, prestige and initiative.

Knight's Cross presentation ceremony for *SS-Hstuf.* Klingenberg, at the Berghof.

Bombs on Belgrade. From the magazine *'Der Adler'*.

SS motorcyclists in Belgrade, April 1941.

Employment of SS cavalry units on the Eastern Front Autumn-Winter 1941-42

by Massimiliano Afiero

On 2 September 1941, *2.Schwadron* was involved in an attack against the position at Sawerchlessesje, about thirty kilometers northwest of Sosny. *SS-Ostuf.* Erich Krell and his platoon led the attack against the village, quickly finding themselves under enemy fire. But instead of falling back, the SS cavalrymen continued to move forward towards a farm from which the shooting was coming. After having neutralized the source of fire, they moved on to the village where several civilians reported the presence of a Soviet cavalry unit a few miles inside the forest.

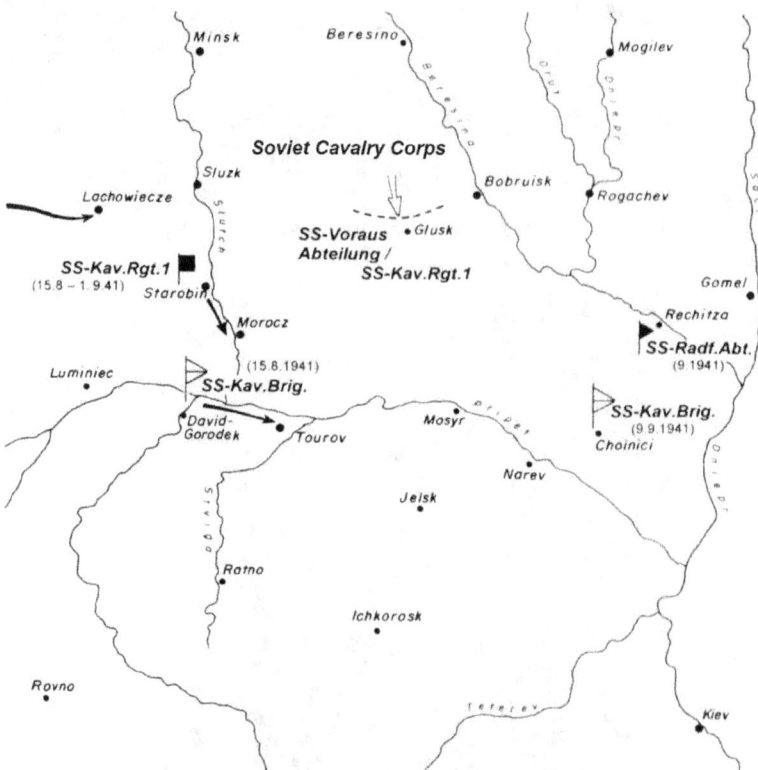

Operations in the Pripet sector, September 1941.

The platoon led by *SS-Ustuf.* Georg Veith took it upon itself to challenge the enemy force, quickly seeking it out. The Soviet cavalry were soon intercepted and following a brief firefight were completely wiped out. During the action, 31 fine horses were seized. Beginning on 30 August, the regiment resumed its march to the east along with other units of *Kommandostab "RF-SS"*, arriving on 6 September along the road that linked Bobruisk and Mosyr and concluding the second cycle of operations in the Pripet Marshes. On 5 September, thirty-six Iron Crosses Second Class were awarded to the men of the brigade, and one First Class to *SS-Stubaf.* Lombard.

SS soldiers during an attack, September 1941.

Continuation of the fight against the bands

During the day of 7 September, the brigade headquarters received orders to carry out new sweeps in the area between the Pripet, Dnieper and the line Retschiza-Ptitsch. *SS-Kav.Rgt.1*, reinforced by the *SS-Radfahr-Aufklärungs-Abteilung*, was to operate on the left flank, while *SS-Kav.Rgt.2* operated on the right. The units quickly reached the assigned objectives, Retschiza for *SS-Kav.Rgt.1* and Mosyr for *SS-Kav.Rgt.2*.

SS soldiers during a break in the fighting, September 1941.

On 9 September, the brigade established its headquarters at Choiniki, while *SS-Kav.Rgt.2* moved to Jurewitschi. This time the orders were to eliminate isolated enemy groups that were attempting to escape from the gigantic Kiev pocket, where huge numbers of Soviet forces had been trapped. On 10 September, an enemy group consisting of around five hundred partisans led by Soviet officers was surrounded near Krasnyi-Ostroff and completely wiped out; at the conclusion of the victorious battle the SS captured 38 Soviet officers, in addition to having eliminated 384 partisans.

September 1941: Himmler visits *SS-Kavallerie-Brigade*. On his right, Kurt Knoblauch, to the left is *SS-Staf*. Fegelein.

Another photo of the visit of Himmler to the SS Cavalry Brigade in September 1941 (*Bundesarchiv*).

Waldemar Fegelein.

The SS cavalrymen suffered no losses! Because of the excellent leadership of this operation, on 11 September, Waldemar Fegelein was awarded the Iron Cross First Class. The sweeps continued into the days that followed, with the partisans who tried to avoid all contact with the brigade breaking up into small groups to better avoid pursuit by the enemy. Avoiding encounters in open territory, they preferred to resist the German actions by using mines and destroying roads and bridges, with the aim of cutting the lines of communication.

Soldiers of *SS-Radfahr-Abteilung*, September 1941.

On 15 September 1941, Himmler and *SS-Brigadeführer* Kurt Knoblauch discussed the future employment of the SS brigades on the Eastern Front; the *Reichsführer* continued to prohibit their use in the front lines because they were still the only units available to provide rear area security and above all he did not want them to lose control over them. The matter was soon made known to *HSSuPF* von dem Bach-Zelewski.

SS soldiers take a meal near their horses as a horsedrawn column of the logistics train passes behind them (*Bundesarchiv*).

On 19 September, the brigade received 96 new replacements coming from *SS-Kavallerie-Ersatz-Abteilung*. On 22 September, with the capture of Soviet General Michael Rumanof and the execution of 42 partisans, operations in the Mosyr area were considered to be concluded.

The brigade was then transferred to the Dnieper-Szos area to eliminate hot spots of resistance there. On 24 September, the SS cavalry units crossed the Dnieper west and south of Gomel, continuing pursuit of the rebel bands and executing several hundred "criminals". On 28 September, units of the brigade were assembled in the Gomel area.

Toropets sector

In early October, the units were transferred by train to the Toropets sector, two hundred kilometers north of Smolensk, to be used to protect the railway line and convoy traffic, subordinated to the *403.Sicherungs-Division* (*Generalleutnant* Wolfgang von Ditfurth). Above all else, the continuous ambushes and sabotage by Soviet partisan bands, whose activities continued to increase, had to be prevented. On 7 October, the brigade headquarters was established at Vitebsk; the same day another twenty-four Iron Crosses Second Class were awarded to the men of the brigade for the earlier actions in the Pripet Marshes. *SS-Hstuf. Willy Plänk*, commander of *1.Schw./SS-Rad.Aufkl.Abt.* received the First Class. The bicycle reconnaissance detachment was engaged during that time to provide security for the Welikije-Luki and Toropets stretches of the railway line, while *SS-Kav.Rgt.2* was engaged in pacifying the area on both sides of the road between those same locations.

SS soldiers in the Toropets sector, October 1941.

During these latest encounters, sixty partisans were killed, among them several women. The SS cavalrymen suffered no losses, while many enemy weapons were captured. On 10 October the brigade moved its headquarters to Toropets, where it was joined on the 12th by the *SS-Radfahr-Aufklärungs-Abteilung* and *SS-Kav.Rgt.1*, to be subordinated to *253.Infanterie-Division* (*Generalleutnant* Schellert). *SS-Kav.Rgt.2* marched to Nevel, arriving at Miesnuiewo two days later, thirty kilometers northeast of the city. On 18 October after a torrential downpour had transformed the road into immense quagmires, the brigade was ordered by *9.Armee* to "pacify" the area crossed by the Welikiye Luki-Rzhev railway line and the Army's boundary area that linked the city of Luschnida (thirty kilometers northwest of Toropets) and the southern shore of Lake Ochwat. Contact was established with *XXIII.Armee-Korps* to bring the operation to a close. The brigade quickly sent out reconnaissance patrols which confirmed that numerous enemy forces were concentrating between the northern flank of *9.Armee* in the area of Jeltzy and the southern flank of *2.Armee* around Lake Ochwat. While the patrols continued to search the area, the bulk of the brigade, with its two cavalry regiments, positioned itself in the northern sector of the area involved in the sweeps. The *SS-Radfahr-Aufkl.-Abteilung* and *Wach Bataillon 705* were engaged in protecting the railway line and the road that led to Rzhev.

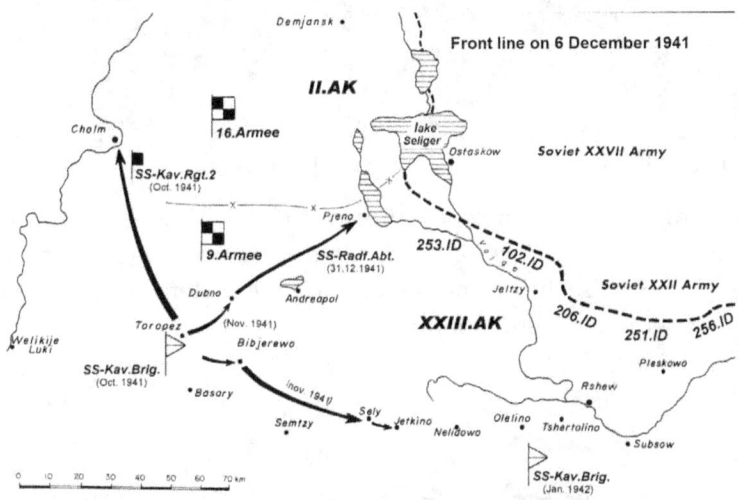

Operations in the Rshew sector, October-December 1941.

German soldiers in a burning village.

On 18 October, the order was received to pacify the northern sector of the *9.Armee* rear area. Good results were achieved until 22 October, before the rains began. On 28 October, the brigade was subordinated to the *Befehlshaber Heeresgebiet "Mitte"*, carryng out anti-partisan operations under its direction.

These SS cavalrymen have discovered a small ammunition cache.

On 31 October, during the course of one of these operations, the SS cavalrymen discovered a small ammunition cache north of Semzy, also capturing some seventy partisans. Soon after, *SS-Kav.Rgt.2* headed towards Cholm, more than forty kilometers northwest of Toropets, from where other sweep operations were mounted.

Autumn 1941. Hermann Fegelein unfolding a map. We recognize Gustav Lombard, holding a cigar in his left hand, and, on the far right, the chief of staff of the *SS-Kavallerie-Brigade*, Karl Gesele (*U.S. NARA*).

Until the beginning of November, *9.Armee* with its *XXIII.Armee-Korps* advanced along both sides of Rzhev, then heading to the north in order to push back attacks by Soviet forces towards the south, departing from their positions between Lake Seliger and Kalinin. *SS-Kav.Rgt.1* left its positions in the forest east of Lugi and moved east towards Okovitzy. Later the regiment was engaged in pacifying the area to the east of Jetkino.

SS-Ostuf. **Willi Plänk interrogates a Russian peasant, Autumn 1941.**

The SS and Russian peasants, Autumn 1941 (*Bundesarchiv*).

An alert was unexpectedly received from the *102.Inf.Div.* whose left flank, located on the large bend of the Volga, found itself under enemy attack. *SS-Stubaf.* Lombard, leading several combat groups formed of army units and those of his own regiment, was able to block the enemy forces. On 6 November, *Generalleutnant* Scheller, commander of *253.Infanterie-Division*, officially thanked *SS-Kavallerie-.Regiment 1* and in particular *SS-Standartenoberjunker* Joachim Boosfeld, leader of one of the cavalry platoons, for having protected his left flank against enemy attacks. That same day the regiment was ordered to secure the Cholmjetzy area. The next day the units took up positions fifteen kilometers north and south of the Jetkino road. From several intercepted enemy radio messages it became known that the partisans were preparing an attack against Jetkino from the south. On 8 November, some elements of the regiment were attacked along the road from Cholmjetzy to Jetkino. Some squadrons were immediately sent as reinforcements in reaction to the partisan attacks against the Jetkino area. The fighting lasted several days at the end of which there were 842 enemy dead.

Employment of other units

From the beginning of November, *SS-Kav.Rgt.2* was kept busy pacifying the area between Toropets and Cholm, where a strong group of partisans and several Soviet paratroop units were quite active. The regiment began to clear the area northwest of Toropets and along the road that connected Toropets with Rzhev. While the units were advancing towards Cholm and had gotten to within about twenty kilometers from their objective they clashed with a partisan formation. In the battle that followed about seventy "rebels" were captured.

Soldiers of the signals company have just come to a halt and the men are warming themselves around a fire (*Bundesarchiv*).

Only one SS cavalryman was killed after having stepped on a mine. On 4 November, another series of sweeps were carried out in the same area, during which another hundred or so rebels were captured. Regarding employment of the *SS-Radfahr-Aufkl.-Abteilung* along with several companies of *Wach Bataillon 705*, the unit was engaged along the road between Toropets and Jetkino, as it was also along the road that connected Schatry and Jetkino, where a partisan formation consisting of at least a thousand men was operating. The recon cyclists later operated in the area northeast of Butaki, destroying numerous enemy support bases and several bunkers in conjunction with the brigade's engineers. On 9 November, the SS cavalry units were deployed as follows: *SS-Kav.Rgt.1* in the Szyoly area, *SS-Kav.Rgt.2* between Pog Potchen and Klimjatina and *SS-Rad.Aufkl.Abt.* near Bibjerewo. During a reconnaissance north of the Rzhev-Toropets road, in the Bibjerewo-Butaki-Dubno area, the SS cavalrymen were able to destroy 24 enemy bunkers and capture 44 partisans. In the days that followed, another 519 partisans were captured. Between 18 October and 14 November, the Brigade claimed 281 partisans killed, 3,018 captured, 141 Soviet soldiers killed and 112 taken prisoner. The SS suffered 7 killed and 9 wounded. On 14 November, by order of the *Reichsführer-SS*, *SS-Kav.Rgt.1*, *SS-Reit.-Art.Abt.* and *SS-Pz.Kp.* were ordered to prepare to return to Warsaw. Nevertheless, the seriousness of the situation at the front forced the units to remain in the rear area. On 15 November, *SS-Kav.Rgt.1* had to move southeast of the area between Jetkino and Berjosa Tal to deal with local partisan activity. The next day, during the course of stiff fighting, 176 partisans were captured. Once that area was pacified the regiment was moved to Rzhev. On 22 November, one of the regiment's platoons was loaded aboard trucks to carry out a punitive expedition along with a motorcycle platoon from the brigade in the area of Tschistowa. During the action a partisan camp was discovered and destroyed. The next day the presence of rebels was reported south of the railway line between Rzhev and Jetkino. The following day the SS units were engaged against other bands to the east of Jetkino while securing the rail line. At the end of the month the SS cavalrymen began to prepare their winter positions, while still carrying out reconnaissance missions to combat the partisan bands, whose activities had intensified significantly following the departure of units of the *255.Sicherungs-Division*. On 27 November, the partisans attacked units of the brigade at Bibjerewo; sixteen partisans were killed in the encounter. On 1 December, in an attempt to improve protection of the position at Jetkino, the brigade's *Flak* battery was transferred there. During the first week of December the SS units were engaged against an enemy band consisting of some two hundred men that was operating in the area northwest of Putiwl. The partisans also had a *PzKpfw III* that had been captured earlier from the Germans. During the actions that followed 73 partisans were killed and 93 captured. For their part, the SS suffered three killed and eight wounded. Also during the second week of December the SS cavalrymen continued to be engaged against other rebel groups; the biggest success was achieved in the forests southwest of Jetkino, where a band consisting of 400 partisans led by Frohmenkoff, a rebel chief who had long been sought by the Germans, was wiped out. Later, the SS units were engaged in securing the stretch of the Welikiye-Luki railway line, which was vitally important to *9.Armee* for its supplies.

Bibliography

Massimiliano Afiero, "*8.SS-Kavallerie-Division Florian Geyer*", Associazione Culturale Ritterkreuz 2010
Charles Trang, "*La Division Florian Geyer*", Heimdal Edition

LAURITS JENSEN
Free Corps Denmark
by Lars Larsen

Laurits Jensen was born on 23 February 1922 in Loekken, Denmark, as the oldest of three siblings. Shortly after his birth, the whole family moved to Arentsminde. When he was young, Laurits Jensen worked at a farm, where he got to know another worker of the farm, Svend Larsen. He was 1½ years older, and had tried to join the Danish Finland Battalion in 1940, but he never made it, as the armistice between Finland and Russia occurred on 13 March 1940. Sven Larsen was among the first, who joined *Free Corps Denmark* in July 1941. There is no doubt that the two young men discussed the situation of the world in the year of 1941.

Laurits Jensen in civilian clothes (*Larsen Collection*).

Laurits Jensen volunteer

Laurits Jensen joined *Free Corps Denmark* (Danish: *Frikorps Danmark*) at the start of December in 1941. He bound himself to a 2-year contract, which expired on 13 December 1943, as he attended military examination on 13 December 1941. On 8 January 1942, he travelled through Gedser to the SS-introductory school in Sennheim, Germany. On 15 February 1942, he was finished at the school in Sennheim, and he was transferred to *Free Corps Denmark*, which was being trained in Treskau. First, Laurits Jensen became a part of the replacement company, and in April 1942, he became a part of *SS-Obersturmführer* Per Sörensen 1st Company. He was there from the beginning, when *Free Corps Denmark* was flown into the Demyansk-Pocket in

Russia on 7 May and 8 May 1942. *Schütze* Laurits Jensen participated in one of the major attacks of *Free Corps Denmark* on 28 May 1942, at the village of Ssutoki.

Frikorps Danmark in the Demyansk-Pocket.

A couple of days before, on the nights of 25 May and 26 May 1942, patrol from *Free Corps Denmark* had made an observation. Russian troops, at the village of Ssutoki, were constructing a bridgehead north of the Robja stream. The patrol also discovered that the Russians had already built bunkers and positions. In other words, the Russian bridgehead was almost ready for a Russian attack.

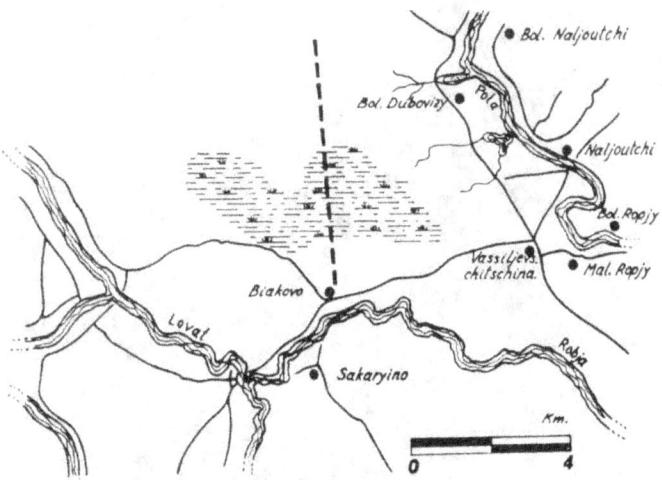

Map of the area of the Demyansk-Pocket.

In the case of a Russian attack, *Free Corps Denmark* could lose 'Rollbahn', which was only 2 kilometers away from the new Russian positions. It would be a disaster for the whole Demyansk-Pocket, if "'Rollbahn'" was lost to the Russians, as it was the only supply route to the trapped Germans forces. The patrol returned to their own positions, early in the morning on 27 May 1942, and quickly reported to *Hauptsturmführer* Poul Neergaard Jacobsen, who was the commander of the 3rd Company of *Free Corps Denmark*. He quickly informed Christian Frederik von Schalburg, the commander of *Free Corps Denmark*. The situation was then discussed and assessed quickly by C.F. von Schalburg, K.B. Martinsen and the other three company commanders, Per Sörensen of 1st Company, Boy Hansen, German, of 2nd Company and Poul Neergaard Jacobsen, 3rd Company.

SS-Stubaf. **von Schalburg.**

Attacking the Russians

C.F. von Schalburg wanted to make a direct attack against the Russian bridgehead, whereas K.B. Martinsen believed that it was a risky maneuver, without even knowing the consequences of a direct attack. In the end, units of 1st Company would attempt to observe the Russians and eventually attack the bridgehead. *Untersturmführer* Johannes Just Nielsen of 1st Company, 2nd Platoon, was chosen to lead the mission. During 27 May 1942, he chose his people for the mission. Johannes Just Nielsen was to advance on the eastern side, and *Oberscharführer* Anton Kern, a German, from the west side. C.F. von Schalburg and K.B. Martinsen had a tactical meeting, and agreed that the units should get as close to the Russian positions as possible, after which they should quickly withdraw. If they had the opportunity, they would neutralize the Russian forces. The engineer platoon of the Free Corps had made some special explosive charges on pipes, and the patrol was handed out extra grenades and ammunition.

SS-Ustuf. **Johannes Just Nielsen.**

The operation had a good start. The group of Johannes Just Nielsen sneaked all the way up to the Russian positions without being detected, and Johannes Just Nielsen judged that an attack was possible. The attack was launched, and a lot of hand grenades were thrown at the Russian positions and shortly thereafter, *Free Corps Denmark* captured the Russian positions, as they entered the trenches and quickly neutralized all the Russians. The attack was a major success of *Free Corps Denmark*, and about 100 Russians had been killed. *Untersturmführer* Johannes Just Nielsen ordered a retreat, but shortly thereafter, the positions were being shelled by 120 mm mortars. The shelling lasted about 10 minutes, after which they were shot at by heavy Russian machine guns.

Soldiers of *Free Corps Denmark* crawled out of the positions and quickly withdrew. Johannes Just Nielsen was about to leave as one of the last persons, when he was shot by a volley from a Russian machine guns. He fell dead in the Robja stream, where they could not retrieve the body. The body is most likely still at that location to this day. *Rottenführer* Gunner Jensen died as well on that day, while five others were wounded.

Photo taken at Ramuschewo, Demjansk Pocket (*Larsen Collection*).

The Iron Cross and the wound

The success was short lived, however, as the Russians had already re-occupied the positions during the morning of 28 May 1942. Laurits Jensen participated in this action, and along with 18 other soldiers of *Free Corps Denmark*, he received the Iron Cross Second Class for his efforts. On 1 June 1942, he was promoted to *Sturmmann*. The majority of the Danish volunteers, who participated in the battles at the Demyansk-Pocket, were at some point wounded. At one point, a shrapnel of a grenade hit Laurits Jensen in his shoulder, which was later surgically removed.

Group of *Frikorps Danmark* soldiers.

I have not been successful in discovering when he was wounded, but during the leave of absence in the autumn of 1942, he gave the shrapnel to his sister as a souvenir, and for many years, the family had the shrapnel displayed. In addition, it is certain that during the leave of absence in 1942, he went to a photographer and got a fine portrait photograph. A picture, which resembles a normal young man of that period, with nicely combed hair and fine clothes. The sister still has the tie, which he wore on the picture. Home for a leave of absence *Free Corps Denmark* was withdrawn from the battles at Demyansk in August 1942, where after there would be a leave of absence.

Group of Danish volunteers, probably in Biakowo or Vassilevschina (*Larsen*).

A leave of absence, which already in the beginning evolved into a disaster. They may have been praised at the start, when their special train arrived at "Godsbanegaarden" in Copenhagen on 8 September 1942. Afterwards, however, the festivities came to a halt, and the rest of the tour across Copenhagen was particularly tense. For Laurits Jensen, his leave of absence was calm, but he could not let go of the war. He had a brought home a difficult task from the Demyansk-Pocket. During the tough battles on 2 June 1942, in which *Free Corps Denmark* had to move the main frontline 150 meters closer to the Russian positions, many soldiers of the Corps fell. Among them was Peder Moerch Pedersen of 1st Company, a comrade of Laurits Jensen. He had the dreary task to inform Peder Moerch Pedersens family, who lived in the village of Vrensted, about 32 kilometers from Arentsminde, about the death of their son on the Eastern Front. During his visit to the parents, Laurits Jensen fell in love with the sister of Peder Moerch Pedersen. The sister loved Laurits Jensen as well, and during his brief leave of absence in Denmark, they became engaged to be married. The parents were excited about this, but at same time sad due to the information Laurits Jensen brought them.

Two Danish volunteers, at the right Leon Langebeck, MIA in Hungary 1945.

Demjansk. Right, Poul Windekilde Hansen.
Middle, Jens Andreas Kristensen.

Back to the Eastern Front

On 13 October 1942, the leave of absence ended for Laurits Jensen and the rest of *Free Corps Denmark*. On 10 November 1942, Laurits Jensen joined the DNSAP of Frits Clausen as member number 48 651. A new front awaited, which was the exact opposite of the front during the summer in 1942. This was winter war against the Russians. *Free Corps Denmark* had been assigned to *1st SS-Infanterie-Brigade*, and at first they were supposed to combat and eliminate partisans. Instead, *Free Corps Denmark* was placed at a part of the front, where a major Russian attack was expected. Christmas Eve in 1942 had a calm start, and the Russians knew that the Germans in particular would like this to be a calm day. The Christmas mail from Denmark had been distributed among the companies. The bunkers were decorated, and the wooden ovens provided warmth in the cold Russian winter. K.B. Martinsen, commander of *Free Corps Denmark*, along with his adjutant, *Obersturmführer* Knud Thorgils, had visited the different companies and wished the soldiers a merry Christmas.

Frikorps Danmark in Copenhagen, September 1942.

Right, K.B.Martinsen. Left, KB Flemming Helweg Larsen.

in World War Two 1939-1945

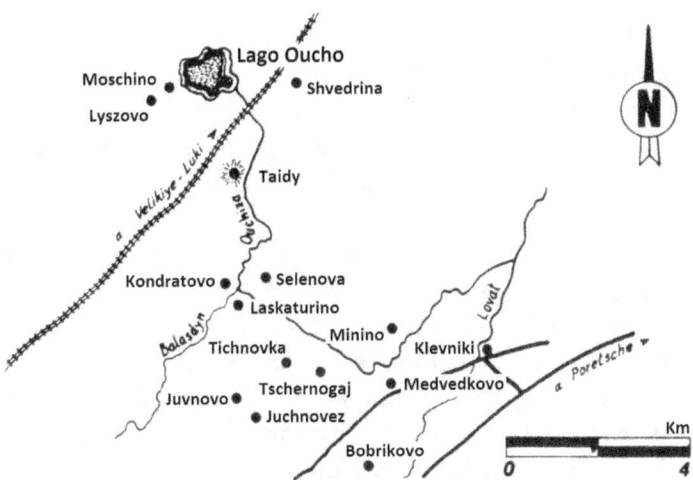

Map of the area of the Velikiye-Luki front, 1942-1943.

However, K.B. Martinsen was worried, as he expected a major Russian attack, and it did not improve the situation that he was located at the headquarter of *Free Corps Denmark*, as he could not be informed about a possible Russian attack. He had forbidden the soldiers to drink of the Christmas spirits, which had been handed out to the soldiers, as they should be prepared for a major Russian attack. K.B. Martinsen and Knud Thorgils trip among the companies was late in the afternoon, as the Russians had a clear view of the snow-covered paths in daylight. At 5 pm, K.B. Martinsen and Knud Thorgils started their trip to the soldiers at the different watch posts and the companies. As the men were very chatty, the trip took a while longer than planned. At 10 pm, they were back at the headquarters, where they finally could enjoy some Christmas dinner, which the creative chefs of *Free Corps Denmark* served, among this a slaughtered pig, which provided them with some good Christmas roasts. The headquarters had been decorated with the Dannebrog flag and leaves of spruce to try to create a nice Christmas spirit.

Group of Danish volunteers in Velikie Luki, Winter 1942/43 (*Larsen Coll.*).

Laurits Jensen falls

It was not quiet for long, however, as the alarm sounded at 11 pm, as large Russian forces launched an attack. Russian infantry, consisting of 200-300 men, attacked the left flank of *Free Corps Denmark*, which also was the place of a unit of *21.Luftwaffe-Felddivision*. The *Luftwaffe-Felddivision* was quickly overrun by the Russians, whereby the 1st Company of *Free Corps Denmark* was left behind in their trapped position. Tough battles raged in particular at the towns of Kondratovo and Laskaturino. There were hand-to-hand battles with fists and bayonets. The 4th Company of *Free Corps Denmark* was in a withdrawn position, compared to the other companies, and the Russians quickly breached the positions of 1st Company. This meant that 4th Company could not provide artillery support, without risking hitting their own soldiers. 2nd Company and its commander, *Obersturmführer* Bent Worsøe-Larsen, had installed themselves in a barn, and was well underway in celebrating Christmas. He was ordered to aid 1st Company as quickly as possible.

Bent Worsøe-Larsen.

Danish volunteers, Winter 1942/43.

Vagn Oest, a telephone operator of 1st Company, had hidden himself in the ruins of a bombed house. From here, he could report on the exact bombing locations to 4th Company. The Russians had neutralized all the soldiers of *Free Corps Denmark*, who were in the ruins, except the telephone operator.

Laurits Jensen, Dog Tag (*Larsen Collection*).

The grave of Laurits Jensen.

Vagn Oest had the only telephone connection that worked, as the rest had been lost. Shortly thereafter, the positions were bombed, while at the same time 2nd Company had arrived there. The battle continued throughout the night, until the Russian soldiers were neutralized at 6 am on 25 December 1942. A couple of hours later, the Russians launched major attack. However, *Free Corps Denmark* was far better prepared this time, but the Russians still got a hold of the outskirts of Kondratovo. It was not until the 26 December 1942 that the remnants of 1st Company could be withdrawn to safe positions. *Sturmmann* Laurits Jensen fell on 25 December 1942, due to several shots in the chest, along with 15 other soldiers of *Free Corps Denmark*.

The French volunteers of the
N.S.K.K. Motorgruppe Luftwaffe
by Christophe Leguérandais

In 1942, with Russian front operations, more and more Germans were drafted into the *Wehrmacht* due to casualties which had become extremely high. Men and resources that once seemed superfluous to victory, now were necessary to hold the front. As a result, drivers and mechanics were badly needed and to fill its ranks, the National Socialist Motor Corps accepted non-Nordics enlistments. The way to the creation of the French section of the N.S.K.K. was opened. In spite of the German occupation of their country since 1940, French citizens became a target for this foreign recruitment, parallel to the L.V.F. or the Todt Organization. The reasons for volunteering were mainly ideological due to anti- Bolshevik propaganda from various collaborationist parties, but some were adventurers, some without political aspirations, attracted by rates of pay and allowances.

In 1942, the N.S.K.K. had paid more attention to the non-Germanic recruits as these Frenchmen in uniform.

For some, the Nazional Socialist Motorized Corps was a stepping stone to join the SS armed forces. When the *Waffen SS* began recruiting members to fight on Eastern Front (authorized in France in 1943), ex-French N.S.K.K. volunteers were candidates. In total during the war, near 2000 men were recruited throughout the country.

Winter 42-43, with the local population in Russia.

From France to Belgium

Even if prior to 1942, a number of Frenchmen had been serving individually in N.S.K.K. units, in July of this year, it became officially recognized by the Vichy Government. The French section recruiting office was located at *"1 rue Godot-de-Mauroy"* in Paris, led by *"Capitaine Troupeau"*, a member of the fringe pro-Nazi party *"La Ligue française"* from Pierre Costantini, ever involved in the L.V.F. project. Even if such organization was to serve the interests of the Reich, he intended to use the N.S.K.K. in order to consolidate his alliance with the German authorities.

June 1943, during the training at Grammont, west of Bruxelles.

The conditions and benefits of enlistment were shortly announced in the newspapers. Recruits had to be French, in good health, and without criminal records.The age limits were set between eighteen and fifty years of age. Those accepted would have pay, indemnities for them and financial arrangements for their families, pensions in case of disability with the existing scales of the German Army. Morevover membership in this unit did not require any prior knowledge of motorized transport or combat experience. After having passed a short medical examination in Paris and signed a contract for the duration of the war, the 150 first recruits that made up the first contingent were sent to Belgium at Vilvoorde. Attached to the *Luftwaffe*, they were assigned to the 4th Regiment N.S.K.K.. Five months of basic training awaited them with German instructors, most convalescents. Men wore the grayish-blue air force uniform with a left collar patch carries the emblem of the N.S.K.K. (the right collar patch was for the rank).

The changing of the guard in Belgium.

Their own arm badge was with the French flag, the Vichy's Francisque (a central battle axe) and "N.S.K.K." in black letters across the top of the shield. Their oval metal ID tag, bore the inscription MOT-GR-L-Ausl KRFTF (*Motor, Gruppe, Luftwaffe, Auslander, Kraftfahrer*). They were also required to swear an oath of allegiance to Adolf Hitler as commander-in-chief. While they were on active service, their mail was dispatched by the German feldpost once it had been stamped with a unit cachet. Normally it would pass through a censor office, usually the one at Frankfurt (using cachets bearing the letter "e") for mail to southern France and the one at Cologne for mail to northern France (using cachets beraing the letter "c"). with a fresh batch of volunteers arriving each week from France to replenish the ranks, including ex-L.V.F. members still soldiers in the *"great Franco-German cause"*, training continued, and in December, two transport companies were merged, established at the Shaffen Airfield and in Diest.

In autumn 1943, during a military parade at Grammont.

in World War Two 1939-1945

Hans Ströhle, commander of the 4th Company, here in Belgium in 1943.

Both were ready for the great adventure, destined behind front line service to the immediate needs of the German war effort, even if victorious conclusion to the campaign appeared not so imminent.

Behind the front lines in Eastern front

The first transports of members embarked by train for Rostov-on-Don (at the disposal of Luftgau Rostow am Don) in January 1943 had arrived in Soviet Union at the mercy of an exceptional Russian winter. Few could have imagined the severity of the weather conditions that they would eventually have to endure. During operations between Stalino and Dnepropetrovsk the Frenchmen were used as lorry-drivers to transport German Army supplies and ammunition. In the end of February, the Second Company was send by train to Lemberg then on the road: 1064 kilometers by Lemberg-Brody-Rowno-Jitomir-Kiev-Poltawa-Kharkov. In the march to the front, some Frenchmen proved themselves incapable of driving the trucks even over short distances without losing large quantities of equipment, sometimes agreed by company commander's orders. Apart from a few idealists, most of the cadres appear to have enlisted primarily to avoid the front, including the men selected to command the unit. Moreover they showed their inability to endure the rigours of the campaign due to their ages and poor rations, lacking in initiatives, instances of their incompetence was numerous. The result of these actions was a breakdown in discipline, reducing the capacity of the final result. On 124 trucks initially, 70 in Osnowa, near Kharkov, only arrived. Left without the usual forceful German involvement and direction that might have saved the company, material quickly dissolved. In end of March, the companies were ordered to reassemble at the training base and were then sent back to Belgium where the commander of the Second Company formed a German small clique for mutual protection against French drivers. The ineptitude of the commander must be seen as a major factor in the collapse of the unit. Indeed, the causes were many, but paramount among them, the increasing hostility between Germans and Frenchmen was marked by a pronounced lack of communications.

Some comrades of the 4th Company in Grammont, before going to Italy.

November 1943, awaiting a train in Bruxelles to be transported to Italy.

The results were further demoralization and greater hatred. In this atmosphere it was inevitable that quarrels saw nearly 300 volunteers (of 600) dismissed and traveled back to France.

In Italy

German military leaders began to restructure the French unit as 2nd Battalion N.S.K.K. *Luftwaffe* of the 4th Regiment, under the command of the *NSKK-Staffelführer* Josef Seigel. The ex-members were amalgamated with new enlisted and successive contingents, and the reorganization saw three 'new' companies called 4th, 5th and 6th.

André Henriot, son of the Vichy's Minister of Information and Berthet, members enlisted in the *Kolonne 443* **in March 1944 in Italy at Pietole.**

For them, strenuous and unpleasant training period started. The first companies were unprepared for such an abrupt commiment in campaign, and accordingly it was necessary to inquire into the reasons for such haste. They received sufficient instructions in weaponry or survival techniques. *"They want to make us SS members?"* reminded a veteran.

As the units were ready for action on November 1943, the battalion was sent to Italy. In January, the troops themselves were divided into 3 companies of ten columns each (*Kolonnen* in German) operating behind German lines throughout all the North of the country.

They worked for the *Luftwaffe*, O.T., sometimes Heere, but never the N.S.K.K.. The stalemate with the Allies along the Italian front, and the successful German defense of Monte Cassino combined with the demands of the Wehrmacht for more material, resulted in the decline of trucks and men. Despite the camaraderie, some of them deserted in Italy and sometimes joined various partisan units.

The *NSKK-Sturmführer* **Hans Ströhle,** *Kompanieführer* **of the Fourth Company, Second battalion in Italy, summer 1944.**

Some recipients of Iron Cross 2nd Class awards in Italy in 1944 with tropical uniforms.

Needless to say the true initial potential of the Kolonnen were only an effective military force in theory in summer despite the fact their Personalausweis were changed against Soldbuch in July. In September, the formation of the *Waffen-Grenadier-Brigade der SS "Charlemagne"* saw progressively the integration of all the Frenchmen fighting on the Axis side: L.V.F., *Kriegsmarine*, *Schutzkommando OT*, and other German paramilitary units, N.S.K.K. included. However, members in Italy won't be touched by this incorporation.

The last months

In December, the rest of the unit was regrouped and sent in Denmark in the airfield of Alesøe, near Odensee and was to be designated as security for the *Messerschmitt* jets which were nor flying for lack of fuel. The companies were divided into 2 groups of 400 men with each a staff. Due to the failure of the German defensive in Budapest, the first group travelled to Hungary at the end of February-March 1945, where men fighting, military necessity. The second group were also sent some weeks after but never arrived and was sent in Austria, where as a consequence end of war stopped its activities. Before concluding, we can say that contrary to the L.V.F. which was a military unit in the hands of French political men (and near a political movement), the French section of N.S.K.K. was only used for military objectives. Don't forget too the other French volunteers in N.S.K.K. units assigned to the Todt Organization, with another uniform, principally operating in France on the Atlantic Wall but also everywhere Germans needed them.

Bibliography

Robert Forbes, *"For Europe"*, Stackpole books
C. Leguérandais, *"Hitlers' French volunteers"*, Pen and sword

The SS-Division Wiking in the Caucasus: Autumn 1942
by Massimiliano Afiero

September 1942: well supported by their artillery, Soviet units returned to carry out attack after attack. Each time, despite heavy losses, the Soviet infantrymen were able to advance and gain a little ground. *SS-Gruf.* Steiner knew that he had to mount another attack, using the last of the tanks of the armored battalion and *SS-Stubaf.* von Hadeln's soldiers: "*...they will move during the night, taking up positions between the Westland and the Nordland*" ordered the *Wiking* commander. The armored battalion had come out of the latest fighting in a very dejected state, there were dozens of dead and numerous damaged tanks. The tanks that could not be repaired were destroyed.

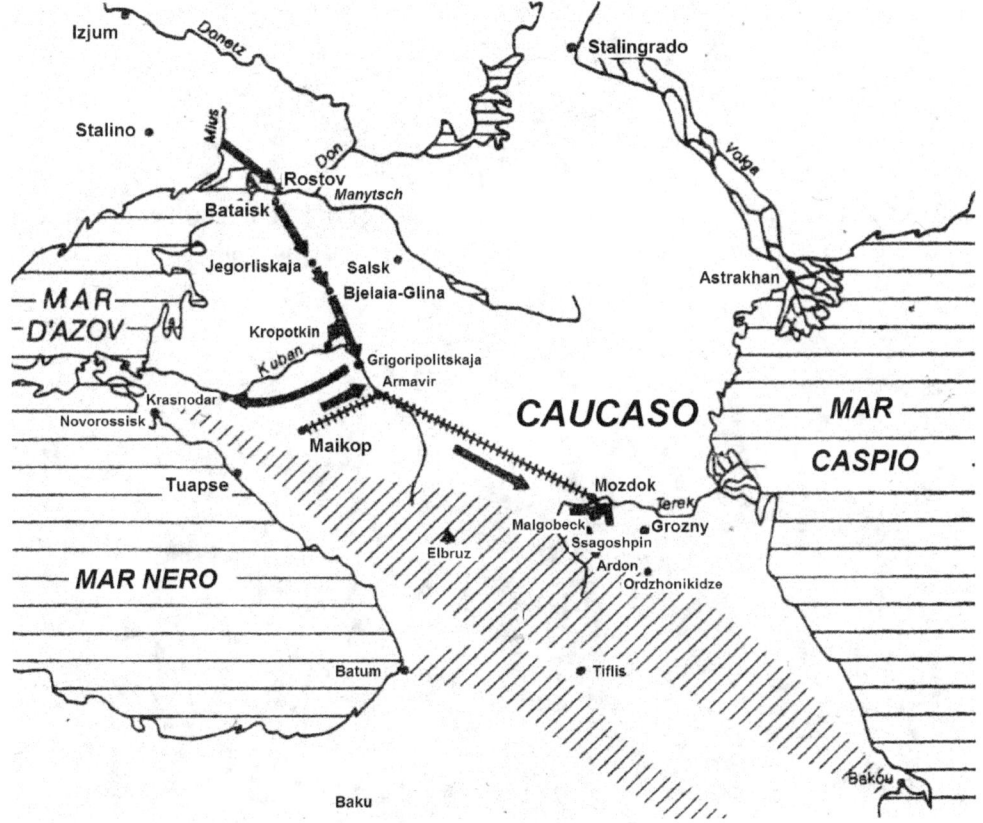

The advance of the *Wiking* in the Caucasus, 1942.

Night and day, the men of the field repair shops, directed by *SS-Ustuf.* Erich Weise, worked ceaselessly to get as many vehicles as possible in working order. The new attack temporarily eased the enemy pressure but did not move the front line forward. Progress of the German forces in the Caucasus was now stalled. This, on the eve of the autumn season, could be considered a real disaster. What worried the officers of the *Wiking* the most undoubtedly was the new attitude of the Soviet soldiers. The Germans now found themselves facing an enemy whose morale was high, well equipped with heavy tanks, aircraft and rocket launcher battalions.

SS-Ustuf. **Erich Weise.**

Resistance was not only courageous and bitter, but also well led. The Soviets had already shown their spirit of sacrifice, but now they knew how to fight as well.

Maintenance of a *PzKpfw.III Ausf.N* by *Wiking* mechanics.

The arrival of the "Germania"

For the time being, the *Wiking* Division had to give up any attack plans, because even in other sectors the units of von Kleist's *Panzerarmee* had not been able to make any breakthrough. The Germanic volunteers accordingly continued to occupy defensive positions south of Malgobeck.

A *PzKpfw.III Ausf. L* of the *Wiking*.

The German command, however, assessed that Steiner's units were stuck too far between enemy lines and that the front line had to be realigned by a new large-scale offensive. *SS-Gruf.* Steiner was puzzled by the realistic possibilities of a new attack. In a meeting with the *Generaloberst*, in answer to a request for reinforcements with which to mount an attack, von Kleist replied that: *"…but with your third regiment, the 'Germania', which has not yet been committed to this front"*. *SS-Staf.* Wagner and his three battalions were expected to arrive the following day, coming from the western Caucasus.

SS-Gruf. **Steiner in a cornfield (*Tiquet Coll.*).**

Panzer and Soldiers before a new attack in the Caucasus, Autumn 1942.

This time the attack was to be made against Grozny. Once that oil region had been conquered, von Kleist hoped to be able to continue his advance to the east and reach the shores of the Caspian Sea. 'Germania' arrived in the sector with two of its three battalions, those of Dieckmann and Jörchel. With them there was also a divisional artillery group. The attack date was fixed for 5 October. As support, SS-Gruf. Steiner provided what was left of the two armored companies, amounting to about twenty tanks in all. The other two regiments of the *Wiking* were also to participate, *Nordland* to protect the southern flank and *Westland* in reserve, ready to join as necessary.

General Ewald von Kleist.

At the same time the reconnaissance battalion under SS-Stubaf. Otto Paetsch took up positions west of Ssagopschin to protect the southern flank of the offensive. On the afternoon of 4 October, all of the unit commanders who were to take part in the new offensive gathered at SS-Staf. Wagner's command post.

A *PzKpfw.III Ausf.J* of *1.Panzer-Kompanie*.

The '*Germania*' commander had also asked for his regiment's small unit commanders to be present. Discussions continued until late at night to iron out all of the details of the operation. On that same day of 4 October, General von Kleist, who was impatient for the *Wiking* to begin to attack, sent the following radio message to *SS-Gruf.* Felix Steiner: "*The whole Army is looking to your division. You have the task of clearing the way to Grozny. I expect your armored spearheads to be in Ssagopschin at 18:00 this day*". During the night between 4 and 5 October, the *Wiking* units assembled in the area in front of the hilly area of Malgobeck.

Soldiers of the *'Germania'* on the hills west of Malgobeck (*Michael Cremin*).

SS-Stubaf. Dieckmann.

The attack against Malgobeck

The attack against Malgobeck began at 4:30 on 5 October 1942. In the lead position were the soldiers of *1.Kp./Germania* commanded by *SS-Hstuf.* Hans Dorr, who a few days earlier, precisely on 27 September, had been awarded the Knight's Cross for having distinguished himself in combat on the Kuban. Most of the unit commanders climbed aboard tanks to get a better view of the battlefield while at the same time acting in close cooperation with their comrades in the tank platoons. To support the attack from the air, the support of a squadron of *Stuka* dive bombers had been laid on. In addition, supporting infantry units consisted of the infantrymen of *Infanterie-Regiment 70 (111.Inf.Div.)* commanded by *Oberst* Tronnier. The two *Gemania* assault battalions, the *I.* and *II.Bataillon*, reached the outlying houses of Malgobeck around eleven, but were stalled by heavy enemy resistance. The panzers, which were stalled further to the rear because of the very rough terrain, were not able to provide any supporting fire. *SS-Staf.* Wagner then radioed a request for *Stuka* support; after about half an hour, about twenty dive bombers appeared and for about an hour devastated the town of Malgobeck. Soon after the air attack, the infantrymen of the *Germania* and of *Oberst* Tronnier mounted an assault against the Soviet positions, engaging in furious close-quarter fighting amidst the smoking ruins of Malgobeck.

Preparing for the attack against Malgobeck: from the left, *SS-Hstuf.* Hack, commander of *III./Germania*, General Ott, commander of *LII.Armee-Korps* and *SS-Stubaf.* von Hadeln of *I./Westland*.

The few enemy survivors of the *Stuka* bombardment fought like devils to the end, contesting the Germans for every foot of ground. It was not until about two in the afternoon that Malgobeck was firmly in German hands. *Germania* counted about thirty dead and more than two hundred wounded. It was a victory bought at a high price, but Wagner could feel satisfied for having succeeded where other German units had failed for days. With the fall of Malgobeck, the Soviets threw several armored formations into the battle along the Grozny road in an attempt to hit the *Germania's* new positions in the flank. Thanks however to intervention by anti-tank units and the infantrymen of *II./Nordland*, the Soviet tanks were forced to withdraw. On 6 October, the German offensive resumed; there was a heavy mist throughout the area that gave the landscape a shadowy appearance, limiting visibility significantly. Following renewed close-quarter fighting, the *Germania's* SS soldiers were able to seize all of the enemy positions east of Malgobeck, including a completely intact oil storage facility.

An SS soldier speaking with a tanker during the attack (NA).

Panzers **from** *1.Kompanie* **of the** *Wiking* **armored battalion.**

An SS soldier drawing ammunition.

The Germanic volunteers had been able to reach the *"Grusinische"* road and to intercept several convoys of American materiel that the United States had sent to the Soviets via the Persian Gulf and Iran. At that point, the offensive thrust of the German units halted once again, because in the meantime the Soviets had been able to move an entire infantry division and numerous rocket launcher batteries into the area.

A rare photo of SS troops from *'Germania'* entering into Malgobeck. (*C. Trang collection*).

in World War Two 1939-1945

On 8 October, the front stabilized once again, with both Soviet and German units assuming defensive postures, consolidating the positions that they had reached: for their part, the *Wiking* units established a continuous front between the villages of Keskem and Malgobeck. That same day, the *Wiking* artillery regiment commander, *SS-Oberführer* Otto Gille, was awarded the Knight's Cross for extreme valor demonstrated in combat.

Steiner awarding the *Ritterkreuz* to Gille.

The inferno on Hill 701

Unhappy with the results achieved by *Wiking*, von Kleist asked Steiner to wrest Hill 701, west of Malgobeck, from the enemy, in order to be able to continue the advance towards Grozny. From its heights, traffic along the Grusinische road could be controlled. For that action, upon personal suggestion by von Kleist himself, the *III./Nordland*, which was the Finnish battalion commanded by *SS-Stubaf.* Hans Collani, was designated. *SS-Ostuf.* Tauno Pohjanlehto, a native of Sunila, took part in the attack with his 9th Company. The hill, strongly defended by Soviet units, was attacked in vain for fully eight days by the Finnish volunteers of the *Wiking*. Among them were many veterans of the Winter War against Soviet Russia and many of them had already fought on the Eastern Front, but no one had ever seen such a hell before. After days and days of repeated assaults, the Finns were still at the foot of the hill, stalled by Soviet barrage fire after having suffered heavy losses; the 9th Company was left with a few dozen men, the 10th and 11th had been merged together to form a single assault unit consisting of about forty men. Only the 12th, the heavy company, was still at full establishment. *SS-Ostuf.* Pohjanlehto had found shelter in an abandoned Soviet bunker along with the remnants of his company; the men were all starving and filthy. During the night between 15 and 16 October, *SS-Stubaf.* Collani dropped into the bunker unexpectedly.

A Finnish defensive position in Malgobeck, October 1942.

SS-Stubaf. **Collani with** *SS-Ostuf.* **Deck.**

SS-Ostuf. **Tauno Pohjanlehto.**

A candle was quickly lit. The Finnish volunteers shifted to make room for their commander, there was nothing to eat, but a bottle of red wine suddenly appeared. The battalion commander reported that the next day there would be a new attack led by Pohjanlehto with the survivors of the Finnish companies, while the company led by *SS-Ostuf.* Mühlinghaus would provide supporting fire with his heavy weapons, mortars and machine guns.

Officers of *III./Nordland* observing the effect of artillery fire against Soviet positions in the Malgobeck area.

Half of a *Wiking* armored company would also be in support. It was decided that the attack would be kicked off without any preparatory artillery fire in order to try to catch the enemy by surprise. At dawn, a thick fog blanketed the valley and the top of Hill 701; after having gathered their arms and equipment the Finnish volunteers prepared to attack the enemy positions for the nth time. After a few minutes, covered by the mist, they reached the edge of the first Soviet trenches, taking advantage of the effect of surprise. *"Forward!"* yelled *SS-Ostuf.* Pohjanlehto with all his might. His men followed him into the attack in the midst of the fog, quickly climbing up the slope. Then the Soviets reacted, shooting down on the Finns. At that moment the German artillery joined the action, which began to shell the top of Hill 701. Down in the valley, the *Wiking* panzers also provided fire support for the action. Hill 701 quickly became a smoking volcano. The Soviet soldiers, most of who were wounded, continued to fight on doggedly nevertheless. Collani's volunteers were soon engaged in hand-to-hand fighting with the enemy. The panzers were called upon to bring the capture of the hill to its conclusion.

Volunteer Antero Lanerva of *10./Nordland* in his trench in the hills near Malgobeck.

But only two tanks arrived, which after having loosed a few rounds against the toughest bunkers, were forced to pull back to escape the Soviet artillery barrage. The Finnish volunteers were thus left to fight for themselves. All of a sudden a Soviet shell landed in the midst of the Finns of Pyyhtiäs' group; many men were killed or wounded and *Sturmmann* Kesti literally flew into the air due to the effect of the explosion. German *SS-Uscha*. Metz had picked up a Soviet hand grenade and while in the act of throwing it back to the sender was hit in the arm by an enemy bullet.

Finnish volunteers of *III./Nordland* prior to the attack on Hill 701.

The grenade fell to the ground, exploding between his legs. Shredded by fragments, the sergeant died a few moments later. Another *Unterscharführer*, the Finn Miettinen, managed to spring into the enemy positions, but when he was about to engage in hand-to-hand fighting, he was hit by a bullet full in the stomach. Before falling to the ground, however, he was able to fire off the entire magazine of his machine pistol, killing at least four or five Soviet soldiers. *SS-Ostuf*. Pohjanlehto looked around the area, he seemed to be in hell; his forehead was hot, his temples were pulsating and his throat was completely tightened. Around him were only men who were wounded or completely paralyzed by fear; enemy bullets whistled past in all directions. To escape the enemy fire, Pohjanlehto and volunteer Sakari threw themselves into a hole. Enemy bullets continued to pass over their heads.

An *MG-34* of *Nordland* providing covering fire.

There was a Soviet soldier In another hole a few meters away. Recovering momentarily from the shock of the battle, Pohjanlehto discovered a large machine gun with a circular magazine on the edge of the enemy trench. He waited a few seconds, and when the enemy soldier tried to get out of his hole, he emptied his whole magazine into the soldier. Soon after that, he rallied his men to attack again; "*Forward!*" he shouted again at the top of his lungs. After having covered a few yards, the Finnish volunteers finally reached the crest of that damned Hill 701, after having destroyed several Soviet anti-tank guns with hand grenades. "*Now our panzers can move up undisturbed*" he was able to report with satisfaction. The *Wiking* panzers were again able to make their way up the slope, straining their engines. Their tracks bit into the ground, throwing up clods of dirt in all directions. *SS-Ostuf.* August Mühlinghaus, commander of *11./Nordland*, also arrived along with the tanks. He brought ammunition, machine pistol magazines and hand grenades with him. With the arrival of the tanks, the Soviet survivors ceased all resistance and came out of their bunkers with their hands raised. The Finnish volunteers were able to capture a lot of equipment from the enemy: anti-tank guns, infantry support guns, heavy machine guns, individual weapons.

A 50mm anti-tank gun engaged in hitting Soviet positions.

In that brief moment of quiet, thoughts quickly went to the wounded and dead. *SS-Ostuf.* Pohjanlehto went to the lifeless body of his company adjutant, *SS-Uscha.* Sahlmann, who had fallen during the assault on the hill. After having been hit, he had enough strength to say a few final words: "*Look, my Finnish comrades, how young Germans die…*". The following morning, the Soviets counterattacked with infantry and tanks in an attempt to recapture Hill 701. The *Wiking* panzers met them with their fire, destroying three enemy tanks and damaging many others.

A Soviet Degtyarev machine gun with round magazine, captured by an SS soldier and being used in the fighting on the Malgobeck front, September 1943.

An attack by Soviet tanks, on the Malgobeck front, September 1943.

in World War Two 1939-1945

An SS defensive position on the Malgobeck front.

A *PzKpfw.III* of the *Wiking* with several soldiers aboard.

A *1.Pz.Kp. panzer* with its entire crew.

The survivors of Collani's Finnish battalion continued to act as supporting infantry for the *Wiking's* tanks, taking part in all of the following defensive actions to fend off the Soviet counterattacks. The *Wiking Flak* and *Pak* guns were unerring against the enemy tanks. The mountain slopes around Malgobeck were soon strewn with the hulks of many knocked-out Soviet tanks. With the arrival of the bad weather season the front stabilized, allowing the Germanic volunteers to take a few days of well-deserved rest after the tough autumn fighting.

Bibliography

Massimiliano Afiero, *"Waffen SS in guerra, Volume I: 1939-1943"*, Associazione Culturale Ritterkreuz
Massimiliano Afiero, *"La SS-Division Wiking nel Caucaso 1942-1943"*, Associazione Culturale Ritterkreuz
J. Mabire, *"La division Wiking dans l'enfer blanc: 1941/43"*, Fayard 1980
Charles Trang, *"Division Wiking, volume 2: Mai 1942-Avril 1943"*, Editions Heimdal

FOREIGN VOLUNTEER LEGION STAMP PROPAGANDA IN THE THIRD REICH
by Rene Chavez

La Waffen-SS vous appelle!

The enlistment of foreigners in the German armed forces was partial successful because of the propaganda provided by the pro-Nazi countries. It was not until the German invasion of the Soviet Union that a substantial number of volunteers from Western Europe participated in the *"Crusade against Bolshevism"*. The Germans and the pro-Nazi groups that existed in Western Europe issued a number of stamps, post cards and posters eulogizing foreign volunteer legions. Much public interest was aroused by those colorful, imaginative, concise, and provocative propaganda postal labels and recruiting posters.

Propaganda Stamps

All foreign Legionnaires were given the same free postal franking privilege as their German comrades, however, special legion postage stamps and labels were used on German military mail. These so-called Legion stamps and labels were printed and issued by Pro-nazi private committees to raise funds that partially supported foreign volunteers. The stamps fell into two general classifications:

Legion labels, printed with no postal value and used as such on "Feldpost" (field post) mail (usually purchased by volunteers and family members).

Semipostal stamps, produced in the country that formed the particular legion. These stamps did have postal value. The term semipostal indicates a stamp with two values on it- the first number is the actual cost of postage, while the second is a surtax, used in this instance to support the volunteers.

Stamps with valid postal values were issued in Norway, France, Netherlands and Croatia. These stamps represented legionnaires as patriots fighting for a unified Europe against communism.

Norwegian semipostal stamp.

Figure 1.

The cover in figure 1 illustrates a legitimate post office semipostal stamp showing a Norwegian legionnaire giving orders. The soldier shows him wearing the Norwegian helmet and uniform. On his left arm is an emblem showing "the cross of Saint Olaf," the symbol used by members of the Quisling (Nazi) party. In the background of the legionnaire stamp are both the Norwegian and Finnish flags. The propaganda value was to encourage members of the Quisling party to enlist in the Finnish forces; however, most volunteers ended up joining the German Waffen SS and wearing SS-Uniforms. The cover was mailed to a volunteer and was censored by German military authorities, with a blue *"Gepruft Feldpostprufstelle"* [Inspected Field Post Examiners Office]. Another set of semipostals printed and officially used for postal mail was the Dutch Legion stamps. Two semi-postal stamps were issued by the Dutch postal administration on 1 November 1942. These semipostal stamps illustrate a Dutch volunteer wearing the German SS uniform. Notice the Germanic-Dutch *"wolf hook"* worn on their collar and the Dutch shield. Both stamps were printed in sheets of one hundred.

Figure 2.

In addition, two souvenir sheets shown in figure 2 were printed showing the same design. The 1st stamp is valued at 7-1/2 (+) 2-1/2Cents, the design is in horizontal format, has a dark red color. The 2nd stamp is valued at 12-1/2 (+) 87-1/2Cents, the design is in vertical format, has an ultramarine color. Both sheets have a Dutch inscription, which reads in English *"Stamp issued for the benefit of the supply funds of the Dutch Legion, 1942."*

Another interesting postal issue was the French Tricolore stamps. In October 12, 1942, Vichy France issued a pair of semipostals honoring the French Tricolore Legion, which was an attempt by the Vichy government to legitimize a military unit to protect French interest. These stamps were issued in sheets of 20 containing two rows of five of the blue stamps, then a single row of five white "albino" stamps with no postal value, followed by two rows of stamps in red. The semipostals have a postal value of 1.20 Francs with a surcharge of 8.80 Francs. The design shows the face of a French soldier wearing a beret and in the background a column of Napoleonic grenadiers marching.

Figure 3.

Figure 3, illustrates a German military cover that was mailed by a French Volunteer who was stationed in the military training barracks in Debica, Poland. The cover has two postal canceled French Tricolore stamps, which were not required on military mail because all field mail was free of postal charge.

Legion Tricolore stamps.

The French Tricolore was formed in June 28, 1942 and was composed of French Eastern Front veterans. It was quietly dissolved after only 6 months in existence. Hitler didn't approve the Legion on transferring into a French governing system. Former members of the *Legion Tricolore* were allowed to rejoin the *French Volunteer Legion*.

Legion Labels

Concerning the Legion Labels, the Germans had no quarrels on having these labels used on military mail. Mainly because there was no postal charge on field mail and because most of the mail came from foreign volunteers and family members who were supporting the Germans. The following countries issued propaganda labels: Flemish, Walloon, Denmark and France. Family members or collectors often arranged for complete sets of these legion labels to be affixed to envelopes, which were canceled to order at *Waffen-SS* recruiting offices. Most of the legion covers that were mailed through the German field post system were censored.

Figure 4.

A Flemish volunteer.

For example, figure 4 shows such a cover that was mailed through the German SS recruiting office. The postal cover is addressed to Feldpost number 07515AP a designated SS-recruiting facility. A SASE (self addressed stamped envelope) was mailed to the "VLAAMISCHE VOORZORGSCOMTIG" (Flemish Charity Committee), Laken-weversstraat 1, Brussels. An SS roller cancel was applied to the stamps. This cover shows a set of four, Flemish Legion Propaganda labels illustrating medieval Flemish Knights. These labels were sold by pro-Nazi sponsors and at local post offices. The legion labels are listed in the Michel German Feldpost Catalogue in the section *"Deutsche Besetzungsausgaben 1939-45"* [German Occupation Issues 1939-45].

Figure 5.

Legion propaganda labels commemorated special military events. A pair of Danish legion stamps was issued to commemorate the memorial service of a fallen leader. The Danish commander Count Christian F. von Schalburg, who was killed in action on the Eastern Front, was one such officer commemorated (figure 5). The vertical se-tenant pairs were sold in blocks of ten by pro-Nazi Danish groups in early September 1943. These labels have a color portrait of von Schalburg in Waffen-SS uniform. The upper label bears the denomination "50" and is inscribed: *"Ved Ofre skabtes Danmarks Ere/C.F.V. Schalburgs Mindefond"* (Our sacrifice created Denmark's honor). It also bears the Danish arm shield on each side of the portrait. The lower label has no denomination but the same inscription with one of the shields bearing the SS runes. In addition the headquarters for the Schalburg fund was at Falkonergaardsvei 11, Copenhagen, (abbreviated "Kbhvn"). This address also appears on the lower label. These labels are very rare.

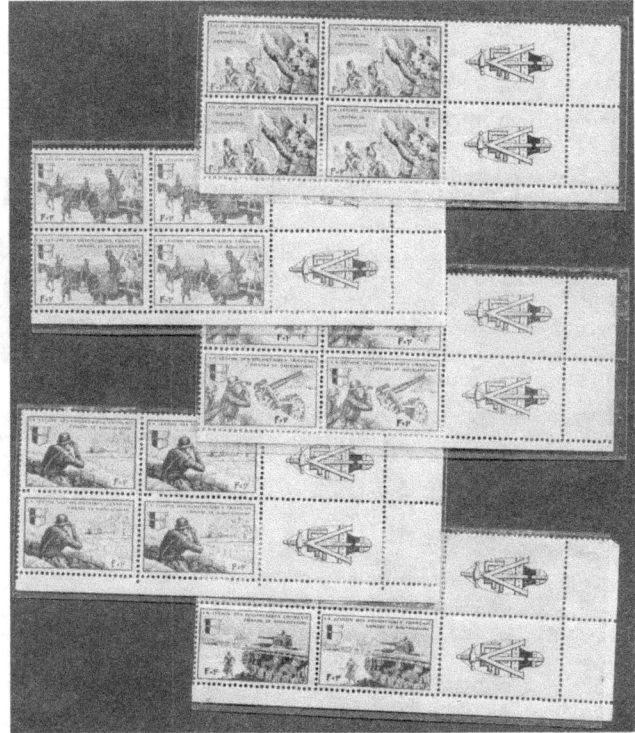

Figure 6.

French volunteers in German service (Signal).

Figure 7: stamps from Flanders.

Figure 8: labels for Galician Division.

Political groups in Vichy France printed many charity stamps to honor the French Volunteer Legion (FVL). Figure 6, shows an interesting set of five FVL labels in blocks of four, illustrating French volunteers in different battle scenes of the Eastern Front. The pictures depict these troops with inadequate winter clothing and modern equipment. One picture shows an obsolete French *Renault* tank, which was no match against the Russian *T-34* Medium tanks. The propaganda was to avenge Napoleon's defeat in Russia by showing Frenchmen at the gates of Moscow. These stamps were issued in 1942 to commemorate the 130th anniversary of the Battle of Borodino during Napoleon's drive towards Moscow. Notice the FVL troops saluting Napoleonic Grenadiers. Not all printed legion labels were issued. Figure 7 shows a striking set of five stamps from Flanders. These stamps showing SS volunteers next to German aircraft were printed but not issued. The majority of Flemish volunteers were drafted into the *Waffen-SS* or used in other military organizations such as the German NSKK aircorps. Legion propaganda stamps were also printed in the eastern liberated countries of Ukraine and Latvia. In September 1943, the Soldiers Welfare Fund in the Ukraine issued a pair of stamps commemorating the Galician Division. The stamps were sold in recruiting and divisional support stations. The stamps in figure 8 show legionnaires in German uniform with the Galician National Shield in the background. The inscription reads *"Riflemen Division SS."* In August 1944, essays were prepared and presented to German authorities but were to late to be taken into consideration as Riga fell to the Soviets in October. The essays illustrate Latvian volunteers and mythical subjects. Four stamps were selected from the 15 stamp designs shown in figure 9.

Figure 9: the essays for Latvian Legion.

Latvian volunteers.

Figure 10: charity labels from the NSAP.

Pro-nazi party groups issued a number of charity labels indicating to some extent that Nazi party members were of Christian faith compared to the atheistic communists. Three Christmas seals with stylized Swastikas from the NSAP (Danish National Socialist Party) are shown in figure 10. Besides stamps or labels, postal cancels with propaganda inscription honoring volunteer legions were used in occupied countries. Illustrated in figure 11 is a French cover from Cannes with a machine cancellation celebrating the anniversary of the French Volunteer Legion. The Norwegian cover in figure 12 has a postal cancel "NORSK FRONT," honoring Norwegian volunteers on the Eastern Front.

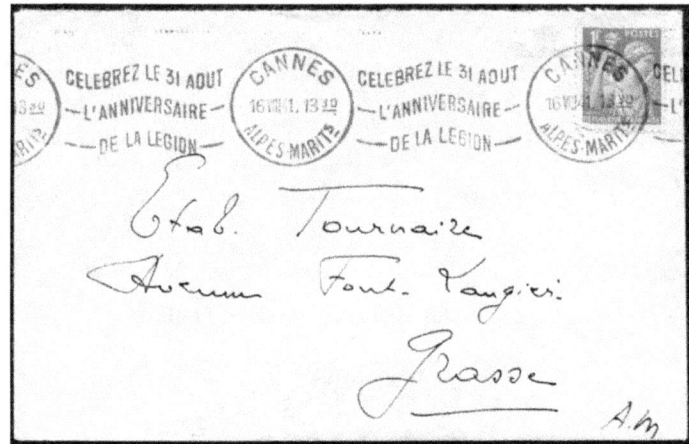

Figure 11.

Figure 12.

Bibliography

Ya Afangulskii, "*THE HOLY WAR AGAINST BOLSHEVISM*", Third Reich Study Group (TRSG) Bulletin No. XXI, October 1987.

Beede, Painter, Harper and Szymanski, "*GERMANY'S FOREIGN LEGIONS*", German Philatelic Society Specialist (GPS), Vol XIX 1968, (Issues 1, 3, 5, 6, 7 & 9).

MICHEL FELDPOST HANDBOOK CATALOGUE, 2nd Edition.

LittleJohn, David, FOREIGN LEGIONS OF THE THIRD REICH, (Vol. I-IV).